ETERNAL REVERBERATIONS 2.0

The Echoes Within

A Book of Poems (2008-2023)

ADITYA VESH PANDEY

ISBN 979-8-89277-668-4

Made with ❤ on the Notion Press Platform

www.notionpress.com

Dedication

To my most precious Avani, Moksha & Kshama…

Thanks for being there. Without you I am nothing…

Contents

BharatVarsh – Oldest Continuously Surviving Civilization

Historical Legends of Bharat

Comprehending Comprehensions

Prologue

Welcome to the world of poetry, where words dance on the fine line between logic and magic, creating a space that allows you to explore the mystical while still anchoring in the rational.

Poetry, for me, has always been a refuge—a language that transcends the limitations of mere logic. As a child, I found solace in the verses that effortlessly expressed the nuances of life, going beyond the confines of straightforward prose.

Traversing through various landscapes, both physical and emotional, I delved into the rich tapestry of folklores and histories shared by my parents and grand parents mostly during my childhood. Fuelling my curiosity, I embarked on a personal quest to validate these tales & legends through my own experiences.

Acknowledging the unique perceptions each one of us holds, I began meeting diverse souls, visiting new places, and documenting my observations. This amalgamation of personal encounters and reflections finds its expression in my poems. Whether it's capturing the essence of my observations about sacred spaces and various other places I have visited or folks I have met, the rhythmic hum of cosmos, Indian folklores, various contemporary and historical events etc. my verses mirror the kaleidoscope of my experiences about this oldest continuously surviving great civilization called Indic Civilization and cover various existential aspects of a human being.

From the intricacies of yoga to contemplations on the creation of the cosmos, my poetry spans the spectrum. It delves into the microscopic world of electrons and quarks, pays homage to historical figures like Adi Shankara, Lalitaditya Muktapida and explores the sacredness of places like Varanasi, Sabarimala, Mato Tipila in US, and the king of temples – Kailashnath etc.

Eternal Reverberations 1.0 was the beginning of my outpouring of my Love and devotion for this great Indian civilization and to the creation and the creator as we know it. Eternal Reverberations 2.0 is the graceful continuation of this sojourn.

The poems within this collection are the echoes of my heart. I hope they resonate with you, connecting your heartbeat to the rhythm of divine. Wishing you a delightful sojourn through the realms of words and emotions.

With love and devotion,

Aadi

टिम टिम टिमकते तारे

टिम टिम टिमकते अंतरिक्ष में कितने सारे ये तारे,
है उत्सव कोई मना रहे या ध्यान मग्न हैं ऋषि सारे।
है छाजाता जब अंधकार तभी तो आते हैं तारे,
अंधकार में सज्जनता का पाठ पढ़ा रहे सारे।
जग रोशन करते हैं सारे!

हैं भिन्न ये जल थल नभ में,
फिर भी सारे हैं तारे।
अनेकता में एकता का गुंजन करते हैं सारे,
यह भेद मिटा रहे सारे!

टिम टिमाते ये युगांतरों और मन्वंतरों से,
मुस्कुरा रहे ये जन्मों और जन्मांतरो से।
इंतज़ार ये करते उसका जो कोइ समझे इनकी चल प्यारे,
चुनौती देते सारे के सारे!

उस ब्रह्म नाद का हिस्सा हैं ये,
सत्यापित सा किस्सा हैं ये,
उस अमरतान की सुर लहरों पर,
त्रुटिहीन तैरता हिस्सा हैं ये।
समझो बूझो जानो इनको , हम सब सारे प्यारे तारे,
टिम टिम टिमकते अंतरिक्ष में हैं कितने सारे ये तारे!

 आदि

Creation and Mysticism

Cosmic Wormholes

In the cosmic tapestry where mysteries entwine,
A concept unfolds, bending space and time.
Wormholes, portals in the vast cosmic sea,
A scientific dance in the fabric of reality.

Einstein's equations, a gravitational ballet,
Predicted tunnels through spacetime's array.
A bridge through dimensions, a cosmic door,
Wormholes, where the laws of physics explore.

In the blackness of space, where nothing seems,
Wormholes emerge in the realm of dreams.
A shortcut through the cosmic sprawl,
A tunnel through which light might crawl.

Through the singularity, where gravity's hold,
Creates a passage, a tale to be told.
A connection between galaxies far,
Wormholes, where mysteries and wonders spar.

Traversable wormholes, a theoretical feat,
A passage through space, where time might cheat.
But exotic matter, a mysterious key,
To keep the tunnel open, a cosmic decree.

Yet in this dance through the fabric of time,
A paradox emerges, a puzzle sublime.
Time travel's embrace, a double-edged sword, T
he past and the future, in tension, are stored.

A loop of existence, where futures entwine,
In the dance of the wormhole, a paradox divine.
A traveller's journey, a temporal leap,
Through the portal of time, where secrets keep.

In the laboratories of theoretical minds,
Wormholes dance, where insight finds.
Quantum entanglements, strings that hum,
In the symphony of spacetime, where wormholes become.

From one point to another, a cosmic fold,
Wormholes, where futures and pasts are told.
A journey through space, a shortcut in the void,
A scientific marvel, where imagination's deployed.

Yet in the quest for knowledge, we tread with care,
For wormholes, a mystery we're yet to declare.
In the cosmic ballet, where wonders spin,
Wormholes beckon, inviting us in.

Through the loop of paradox, where time takes flight,
A journey unfolds in the cosmic night.
Wormholes, the gateways to the unknown,
In the dance of existence, where mysteries are sown.

 Aadi

Higgs-Boson – The God Particle

In the tapestry of particles, a quest unfolds,
A search for truths, where mysteries are told.
Higgs-Boson, the elusive, the God-particle's name,
In the world of physics, where laws proclaim.

Beneath the Swiss and French landscape's grace,
Lies CERN, where particles find their space.
In the Large Hadron Collider's colossal might,
Particles collide in the quest for light.

Sixty-five meters below the Earth's crust,
A subatomic dance, a scientific thrust.
Protons accelerated at the speed of light,
In the pursuit of Higgs, where insights ignite.

Higgs field, an invisible cosmic sea,
Particles wade, gaining mass with glee.
The God-particle, a key to the cosmic code,
In the Higgs field's embrace, where forces erode.

A boson emerges, a fleeting trace,
In detectors' dance, in the collider's space.
Massive detectors, CMS and ATLAS,
Capture the dance of particles so callous.

On July 4, 2012, the announcement rings,
Higgs-Boson discovered, the joy it brings.
A five-sigma certainty, a scientific elation,
In the world of particles, a cosmic foundation.

Nobel laureates celebrate, a triumph profound,
Peter Higgs and Satyendra Nath Bose, renowned.
Higgs-Boson, the key to mass, in physics crowned,
A field of energy, a cosmic glue profound.

The God-particle's existence, a scientific feat,
Validating the Standard Model's heartbeat.
A field of mass, a cosmic ballet,
Higgs-Boson's dance, in the particle array.

In the quantum dance, where mysteries align,
Higgs-Boson's discovery, a scientific sign.
Particles gain mass, in the cosmic sea,
In the realm of physics, where knowledge is free.

So in the world of particles, in the collider's spin,
Higgs-Boson's presence, a triumph within.
A factual journey, a scientific rhyme,
In the exploration of particles, where mysteries chime.

 Aadi

Naughty Quirky Quarks

In the quantum dance, where particles play,
Quarks emerge, in the cosmic array.
Fundamental dancers, in the atomic scene,
In the quantum realm, where mysteries convene.

Quarks, the building blocks, in a cosmic trance,
A trio of flavours, in the quantum dance.
Up and down, charm and strange,
Quarks in pairs, in particles arrange.

In the Vedas' verses, where ancient wisdom sings,
Quantum echoes in cosmic strings.
Upanishads whisper of the cosmic sea,
Where quarks may dance in unity.

Puranas speak in mystical tones,
Of quark-like realms where knowledge intones.
A funny dance in the quantum domain,
Particles whimsical, in a cosmic refrain.

In the quantum cauldron, where reality bends,
Quarks and leptons, cosmic friends.
Mysteries profound, in particles small,
Quantum laughter, in the cosmic hall.

Upanishadic riddles, a quantum twist,
In the dance of quarks, where reality's kissed.
Particles spinning, in cosmic delight,
A mystical realm, in the quantum night.

In the Vedas' hymns, a quantum rhyme,
Quarks and strings, in the cosmic time.
Ancient scriptures, a cosmic guide,
In the quantum dance, where realities hide.

Funny quarks, in the quantum parade,
Charming and strange, in the cosmic cascade.
Particles whimsical, in the cosmic theme,
A quantum comedy, in the poet's dream.

Lord Shiva, the cosmic dancer's embrace,
In the dance of quarks, a mystical grace.
Nataraja, the Lord of the Cosmic Ring,
In every particle, his presence sings.

In the dance of particles, quarks align,
In Shiva's cosmic dance, the divine.
A connection profound, in the quantum scheme,
Quarks in the dance, where Lord Shiva's dream.

So in the quantum dance, where mysteries unfold,
Quarks in the cosmic story, a tale to be told.
In the dance of particles, where realities swirl,
A quantum realm, where the mystical and funny twirl.

 Aadi

Eccentric Electrons

In the dance of atoms, a tale unfolds,
Electrons, the dancers, in orbits they hold.
Tiny particles with a charge so light,
In the quantum realm, where mysteries ignite.

In ancient Indian texts, the echoes ring,
In scriptures, Vedas, where wisdom springs.
Electrons, not by name, but in essence's code,
A dance of energy in the cosmic abode.

In Upanishads' verses, where knowledge blooms,
Mentions of energies, where the universe looms.
Particles unseen, in the cosmic dance,
A dance of electrons, a cosmic trance.

Vedic hymns whisper of energies profound,
In the dance of particles, where echoes resound.
Not electrons named, but the essence they bear,
In the cosmic tapestry, where truths declare.

In the quantum world, electrons play,
Around the nucleus, in a ballet.
Negative charges in orbits arrayed,
A dance of energies, in the quantum shade.

A scientific journey, electrons' tale,
In atoms and molecules, where forces prevail.
Charge and mass in a delicate blend,
In the subatomic world, where realities bend.

Around the nucleus, they tirelessly spin,
In energy levels, a dance to begin.
Quantum leaps in orbits high,
Electrons' movements, a cosmic sigh.

In ancient echoes, a subtle trace,
Wisdom transcends time and space.
Electrons dance, in the quantum stream,
A cosmic ballet, in the poet's dream.

So in the dance of particles, ancient and new,
Electrons twirl, in the cosmic view.
A factual journey, in the quantum theme,
In the dance of electrons, where science gleams.

 Aadi

Kaala – An Enigmatic Dimension of Darkness and Time

In the tapestry of existence, where cosmic rhythms chime,
Resides the enigma of Kaala, a dance beyond our time.
A word that weaves through ages, a tale both dark and bright,
Kaala, the cosmic weaver, draped in the fabric of the night.

Kaala, the silent river, flowing through eternity,
A current of moments, shaping our destiny.
In the canvas of the cosmos, painted black and deep,
Kaala whispers legends, in the silence, secrets seep.

Dark as the boundless heavens, where stars in silence gleam,
Kaala, the eternal night, an endless cosmic dream.
Time, a fleeting shadow, in Kaala's timeless hand,
A dance of birth and death, across the cosmic strand.

In the mystic verses, where ancient scriptures sing,
Kaala, the cosmic dancer, wears time as a wing.
Lord Shiva, the embodiment, in meditation deep,
Kaala's cosmic secrets, in his consciousness, seep.

Shiva, the Nataraja, in the cosmic dance so grand,
Time, a cosmic rhythm, held in his divine hand.
In the sacred verses, where mantras softly hum,
Kaala, the cosmic heartbeat, in every atom's drum.

Dark as the cosmic void, where universes unfold,
Kaala, the infinite canvas, where stories are told.
In the labyrinth of existence, where destinies entwine,
Kaala, the cosmic architect, crafts the grand design.

In the stillness of meditation, where silence is the key,
Kaala, the formless essence, in every mystery.
A paradox of existence, both ancient and new,
Kaala, the cosmic pulse, in every heartbeat true.

So, in the dance of time, where past and future meet,
Kaala, the cosmic conductor, orchestrates the beat.
In the cosmic symphony, where stars and galaxies stream,
Kaala, the eternal dark, an unfathomable dream.

Aadi

Shakti

In the cosmic dance where galaxies twirl,
A force unseen, a mystical swirl.
Shakti, the essence, energy untamed,
In the heart of the universe, she's named.

A dance of power, dynamic and free,
Waves of strength through eternity.
Adi Parashakti, the primal source,
In her, the universe takes its course.

Amidst the stars and celestial fire,
She embodies all that we admire.
The consort of Shiva, a cosmic pair,
In the dance of creation, they declare.

Devi, the Goddess, supreme and bright,
In her, all forms of divinity unite.
Durga, Kali, Parvati, and more,
Each a facet, her cosmic lore.

From Baghor's stone to ancient lore,
In Paleolithic whispers, she did soar.
Triangles and yantras in mystic art,
Shakti's presence from the start.

The sonorous hymns, the temple bells,
In her name, devotion swells.
Protectress, provider, in every prayer,
Shakti's grace, the souls declare.

Smartly woven in Advaita's thread,
Unity in diversity, widely spread.
A synthesis profound in every creed,
In Shaktism's garden, all hearts feed.

In South India's embrace, Amman's might,
Local communities, her guiding light.
From the ancient past to present's glow,
Shakti's dance, an eternal flow.

In energy, ability, a cosmic dance,
Shakti's essence, a divine trance.
A goddess supreme, in every part,
Embodied in the soul, the beating heart.

 Aadi

Mantra

In the realm where silence meets the divine,
A sacred utterance, a celestial sign.
Mantra, the mystic melody of the soul,
A symphony that makes the spirit whole.

Aum, the seed syllable, a cosmic hymn,
Resonating through realms, where lights are dim.
The primal sound, the first in Hindu lore,
Echoing the essence of the cosmic core.

Gayatri Mantra, a radiant prayer,
Bathing the mind in wisdom's golden glare.
Hare Krishna's chant, a melody of love,
Soaring on the wings of the skies above.

Om Namah Shivaya, a sacred vow,
Whispered by seekers in moments of the now.
Mani mantra, jewel in the heart's embrace,
Unveiling compassion, showering grace.

Mantra of Light, a beacon in the night,
Guiding seekers toward the infinite light.
Namokar Mantra, a hymn of humility,
Echoing in the chambers of divinity.

Mūl Mantra, a fundamental rhyme,
Echoing through the corridors of space and time.
Mantras, linguistic ladders to the divine,
Each syllable a step, a sacred sign.

Japa, the rhythmic dance of repetition,
A meditative journey, a sacred expedition.
Prayer beads counting blessings, one by one,
In the cosmic dance, where all is spun.

In Jain, in Buddhist, in Hindu lore,
Mantras echo, the heart's inner door.
Sikhism's hymns, in praise they sing,
A harmonious chorus, a celestial wing.

In the tapestry of traditions, varied and wide,
Mantras weave, in their sacred stride.
Initiation, a key to the mantra's door,
Unlocking realms unseen, forevermore.

Yet, some mantras need no sacred seal,
Open to all, like a love that's real.
Musical, uplifting, spiritually profound,
In every whisper, in every sacred sound.

In the rhythm of life, where mantras play,
A divine symphony, guiding the way.
Through boredom's veil, their essence gleams,
Mantras, the whispers of eternal dreams.

 Aadi

Tantra

In the loom of existence, where threads entwine,
A sacred weave, a path divine.
Tantra, the ancient art of cosmic dance,
A mystical tapestry, a sacred trance.

Warp and weft, in patterns unseen,
Tantra's secrets, like dreams between.
Spread across the fabric of sacred rites,
A symphony of mantras, cosmic lights.

To extend, to spread, a cosmic plan,
Tantra unfolds, the essence of man.
A system, a doctrine, woven with care,
Threads of wisdom in the cosmic air.

In Hindu realms, the Mantramārga's song,
A path of mantras, where seekers belong.
Guhyamantra whispers secrets deep,
In the silence, where cosmic truths seep.

Buddhist Vajrayana, a tantric flight,
Ideas and practices bathed in light.
Indo-Tibetan whispers, Shingon's embrace,
Tantra's influence, in every sacred space.

Beyond Vedic whispers, in Jain's sacred lore,
Tantra's touch, the soul to restore.
In Tibetan Bön and Daoism's grace,
The loom of Tantra, in every sacred place.

Puja, a tantric dance, a sacred prayer,
In temple rituals, the essence rare.
Tantras, Āgamas, Samhitās in prose,
Texts that guide where cosmic wisdom flows.

To extend, to spread, the threads of thought,
Tantra's legacy, in teachings sought.
A loom of words, a philosophical art,
In Tantra's embrace, all religions start.

Colonial echoes, a term redefined,
Tantra's essence, in threads entwined.
Warping traditions on history's loom,
Colonial shadows in Tantra's room.

In Rigveda's hymns, the term is spun,
Tantra's journey has just begun.
Principal part, the main design,
Tantra's secret, a sacred sign.

In Buddhism, Hinduism, Jainism's light,
A bibliographic category, woven tight.
Sutra and Tantra, like threads they twine,
In the cosmic loom, the sacred design.

 Aadi

Yantra

In the sacred realm where mystic whispers sing,
Where ancient knowledge takes celestial wing,
A Yantra blooms, a cosmic design,
A sacred engine, a gateway divine.

Geometry woven in threads of thought,
A cosmic blueprint, a rhythm sought,
Upon the altar of devotion laid,
In temples' hush or homes' serene shade.

Triangles dance in divine embrace,
Circles and squares find their sacred space,
A symphony of lines, a mystic trance,
In the Yantra's embrace, spirits dance.

In temples adorned with Yantras rare,
Deities bask in the patterns' glare,
A sacred language, etched in grace,
Whispers secrets of the cosmic chase.

Oh, Yantra, bearer of sacred vows,
In meditation, your power arouse,
A portal to realms beyond our sight,
Guiding seekers through the cosmic night.

Journey through realms, both near and far,
Unlocking doors to the avatar,
Mystical patterns, each line and bend,
Guide the soul toward its cosmic end.

In Yantra's grace, meditation thrives,
Where sacred energy forever thrives,
A tapestry of the cosmic flow,
In Yantra's embrace, enlightenment's glow.

In homes adorned with patterns profound,
Aesthetic beauty, energies unbound,
Yantra, a talisman, a sacred key,
Unlocking doors to the soul's decree.

Beneath the stars, in silence profound,
Yantra, a mystic mandala, is found,
A sacred dance of shapes and lines,
A gateway where the divine aligns.

In Yantra's embrace, the seeker knows,
A cosmic symphony that eternally glows,
A sacred machine, a celestial chart,
Guiding the journey of the seeking heart.

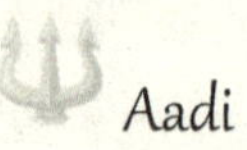 Aadi

Sacred Spaces

Varanasi – A City Since Eternity

In the heart of the ancient land,
Where time and divinity entwine.
Kashi stands, where legends unfold,
A sanctified space, a story untold.

Founded by Shiva, in mystical lore,
His royal palace, forevermore.
A city of three worlds, divine,
Kashi, the cosmic design.

Maha-samashana, the great cremation ground,
Life and death, in balance profound.
A celebration of the inevitable,
In Kashi's embrace, all is memorable.

Vishwanath Temple, a celestial hymn,
Jyotirlinga's grace, where souls begin.
Mahabodhi at Bodhgaya's side,
Where Buddha meditated, enlightenment's tide.

Buddha's sermon in Sarnath's air,
Near Kashi's banks, a spiritual lair.
Art, culture, and music's birth,
Kashi, the cradle of creativity's mirth.

Saints, poets, and philosophers profound,
In Kashi's realm, their wisdom crowned.
Kabir, Ravidas, voices of Bhakti's song,
In Kashi's echo, they belong.

Ganga's embrace, a boat ride divine,
Candlelit prayers on the sacred shrine.
Waves of pilgrims, a holy dip,
Meditation and prayer along the Ghat's script.

As the sun bows to the Ganga's flow,
Evening's art unfolds in radiant glow.
Ganga Arati, a hymn to the divine,
Kashi's essence, in every line.

In the sacred walk with Isha's grace,
Kashi Krama, a spiritual embrace.
Vishwanath, Kalabhairava, temples stand,
A journey transformative, in this ancient land.

Sarnath's peace, where Buddha spoke,
Whispers of enlightenment, sacredly evoke.
Kashi Krama, not a mere pilgrimage's chance,
But a soulful dance in the spiritual expanse.

As Sadhguru says, in the east's holiest domain,
Kashi, the core, where universes remain.

Aadi

Ellora – Symphony in Stone

In Maharashtra's embrace, where time stands still,
Ellora's caves, a testament to skill.
A historical dance, in stones unfold,
The tale of Ellora, timeless and bold.

Amidst the Deccan's rugged terrain,
Ellora's beauty, a timeless gain.
Chisels embraced, in skilled hands they swayed,
Crafting in stones, history portrayed.

From ancient caves, a chronicle told,
Chiselled in basalt, a story unfolds.
Buddhist, Hindu, Jain in symphony,
Ellora's caves, a divine trinity.

Ellora's caves, a symphony in stone,
Chronicles of faith in each carved zone.
In Maharashtra's heart, a treasure untold,
Ellora's saga, magnificence unfold.

Caves 1 to 12, in quiet repose, Buddhist viharas,
where enlightenment chose.
Carved in the rock, monks found their retreat,
In Ellora's embrace, serenity sweet.

Cave 16, Kailasa, a marvel untold,
Shiva's cosmic dance, in stone it's scrolled.
Carved from top down, a mountain transformed,
Engineering marvel, in history warmed.

Caves 30 to 34, in Jain splendor,
Monastic retreats, each chamber tender.
Detailed carvings, of Tirthankaras divine,
Ellora's art, through the annals shine.

Historical whispers of Yadav's reign,
Ellora embraced, their cultural gain.
Centuries witnessed, a vibrant blend,
In stones of Ellora, tales transcend.

Centuries passed, and neglect took hold,
Maratha rulers, restoration bold.
Ellora revived, from time's cruel wear,
A testament to art, a legacy rare.

In Maharashtra's heart, where echoes reside,
Ellora's symphony, a timeless guide.
A treasure trove, in basalt's embrace,
Ellora's saga, an eternal grace.

 Aadi

Kailashnath Temple – A Devotional and Engineering Wonder

By the banks of the Ella, a sacred stream,
Where whispers of history softly gleam.
Ellora Caves, where tales unfold,
A saga of time, in stone, retold.

In Ellora's embrace, a marvel untold,
Kailashnath Temple, a tale to unfold.
Carved from the mountain, top-down divine,
A testament to art, a sacred design.

Hewn from the rock with precision and grace,
A symphony of stone, a sacred space.
Flawless engineering, a mystery untold,
In Maharashtra's heart, where legends unfold.

From the chisel's dance to the sculptor's dream,
A temple emerges, a celestial gleam.
Kailashnath, in Ellora's deep embrace,
An engineering marvel, a timeless grace.

Top-down creation, a mystical feat,
No mortal hands, this divine retreat.
The mountain yields to the sculptor's skill,
A masterpiece carved with a sacred will.

No secrets revealed, no technology named,
Yet Kailashnath's glory remains untamed.
A sanctuary of stone, where echoes reside,
In the heart of Ellora, where mysteries hide.

Columns rise like ancient trees,
Carved gods and goddesses, with such ease.
Shiva's abode, in majestic form,
A celestial dance in every stone's norm.

Pillars, galleries, a sacred abode,
Carved out of Ellora's historic code.
Each nook, each cranny, a divine verse,
In Kailashnath's temple, blessings immerse.

Stone panels whisper tales of old,
Ramayana and Mahabharata unfold.
Inscribed with beauty, etched with grace,
Hindu epics captured in a timeless embrace.

Proof on the walls, our history defined,
Ramayana, Mahabharata, in stone enshrined.
Ellora's caves, a cradle it seems,
Of Hindu civilization's southern dreams.

Wonders of the world, it rightfully claims,
A shrine of devotion, where eternity flames.
Maharashtra's gem, in Ellora's array,
Kailashnath Temple, where gods find a way.

In the hush of the cave, where echoes linger,
A historical hymn, where spirits trigger.
A timeless journey through sculpted halls,
Kailashnath's temple, where divinity calls.

A wonder carved by hands unknown,
In Ellora's realm, a masterpiece grown.
Kailashnath, in Maharashtra's story,
An eternal ode to divine glory.

 Aadi

Ajanta Caves – A Timeless Marvel

In Maharashtra's embrace, where echoes dwell,
Ajanta's caves, a historic spell.
A tale in stones, where time stands still,
Ajanta's symphony, a Marvelous thrill.

Amidst the Sahyadri's gentle embrace,
Ajanta's caves, a sacred space.
Chisels in hand, artisans profound,
Carved in rocks, history unbound.

From the 2nd century, a saga begun,
Buddhist sanctuaries, each a sun.
Caves one to nine, a tranquil retreat,
Monastic life, in rock's heartbeat.

Ajanta's caves, in history's embrace,
Echoes of art, a sacred grace.
In Maharashtra's heart, a treasure unfold,
Ajanta's symphony, a story told.

Cave 16, a muralist's delight,
Ceiling adorned, with colours bright.
Bodhisattvas and celestial lore,
Ajanta's canvas, an ancient core.

Transformation echoed in the caves,
Hinayana to Mahayana paves.
Buddha's teachings, on stone displayed,
Ajanta's essence, through time conveyed.

Ajanta's caves, in history's embrace,
Echoes of art, a sacred grace.
In Maharashtra's heart, a treasure unfold,
Ajanta's symphony, a story told.

Gupta dynasty's reign, a golden age,
Ajanta's glory, history's page.
Caves painted, in vibrant hues,
Dynastic pride, in the art it strews.

Centuries passed, the caves concealed,
Nature's cloak, their beauty sealed.
1819, a British officer's gaze,
Ajanta rediscovered, in a historic blaze.

In Maharashtra's hills, where silence weaves,
Ajanta's beauty eternally cleaves.
A timeless dance, in rocks engraved,
Ajanta's elegance, in history saved.

 Aadi

Hampi – A Sacred Tale on Stones

In Karnataka's embrace, where boulders stand,
Hampi's tale echoes, a storied land.
Yet, history's pages bear a scar,
When invaders came from lands afar.

Warriors on horseback, a thunderous sound,
As Hampi's soil shook, the battleground.
Invaders came with a ruthless might,
A city's resilience put to the fight.

Vijayanagara, once a beacon bright,
Now faced the invaders' brutal might.
Columns that once held the royal gaze,
Became witness to the city's phase.

Hampi's ruins, where echoes reside,
A city's tale in stones, far and wide.
In Karnataka's embrace, where memories bloom,
Hampi, an ancient, silent, and storied tomb.

In the aftermath of a brutal siege,
Hampi's empire faced a somber intrigue.
Pillars crumbled, temples laid bare,
The city wept in a silent prayer.

The Virupaksha temple, once vibrant and grand,
Now stood amidst the invaders' command.
Hampi's bazaars, a silence profound,
As the invaders roamed the sacred ground.

Hampi's ruins, where echoes reside,
A city's tale in stones, far and wide.
In Karnataka's embrace, where memories bloom,
Hampi, an ancient, silent, and storied tomb.

Kishkindha of old, in Rama's tale,
Ancient whispers, where monkeys set sail.
Pampa's deity, in the city's core,
Hampi, Pampakshetra, forevermore.

Yet, as the sun dipped on Hampi's despair,
A resilience in the stones lingered in the air.
The Tungabhadra, a solace so deep,
Whispered tales of the city's sleep.

On Malyavanta's hills, where sunsets weave,
A tapestry of colors, in the eve.
Matanga's hill, at the dawn's first light,
Sunrise whispers away the night

In Hampi's silence, a city's lament,
Yet, through the ruins, resilience is sent.
A testament to time, Hampi's enduring might,
A phoenix rising in history's silent night.

 Aadi

Grace of Dhyanalinga

In the heart of silence, where words dissolve,
Dhyanalinga stands, a sacred resolve.
A union of dhyana, meditation's grace,
And linga, the form, in a hallowed space.

No creed it follows, no rituals to bind,
Dhyanalinga's realm, a sanctuary of the mind.
Sadhguru's creation, a dream divine,
A portal to the sublime, where energies entwine.

Three years of prana pratishtha's dance,
Locked chakras, in a mystic trance.
A live Guru's presence, an intimate chance,
Dhyanalinga beckons, in its sacred expanse.

A doorway to enlightenment, liberation's call,
In its presence, the soul enthralls.
No prayers, no worship, no need to plea,
Just silent sitting, a communion with the free.

Gaze upon the linga, a powerful sight,
Close your eyes, palms open, bathed in light.
No concentration needed, no struggle to find,
In Dhyanalinga's sphere, a tranquil mind.

An offering of oneself, the purest key,
To unlock the energies, to set the spirit free.
Chandrakund and Suryakund, a sacred pair,
Enhancing receptivity, in the divine air.

Bell chimes every fifteen, a sacred sound,
Enter and exit in the silence profound.
Fifteen minutes, a gift to your soul,
In Dhyanalinga's embrace, let serenity enroll.

Nada Aradhana, a symphony divine,
Twice a day, where sound and spirit entwine.
Vocals flowing, instruments in play,
Enhancing the journey in the mystic array.

Inexplicable bliss, an evolution's dance,
A transformation swift, a soul's advance.
Life's perspective shifts, in the silent core,
Dhyanalinga's grace, forevermore.

Sadhguru, the guide, the heart's thanksgiving,
Isha Foundation's embrace, a soul's living.
In the sanctuary of Dhyanalinga's grace,
A journey unfolds, in the divine space.

 Aadi

Linga Bhairavi Devi – Divine Feminine

In the sanctum of cosmic energy, a linga takes form,
Linga Bhairavi, where the divine weaves a storm.
Consecrated by Sadhguru's prana pratishtha's grace,
A manifestation of the divine feminine, a sacred space.

In the dance of creation, Devi's essence weaves,
Fierce and compassionate, in every soul she cleaves.
Ultimate proportions, a form so rare,
Linga Bhairavi, a goddess beyond compare.

With three and a half chakras, her energy unfolds,
Mooladhara, Swadhishthana, Manipuraka, stories untold.
Anahata, the heart, a sacred fold,
In Devi's abode, mysteries manifold.

Oh, Linga Bhairavi, in devotion we find,
A million ways, your grace intertwined.
If hearts melt with love's art,
Devi yields, playing her part.

In the geometry of the sacred, symbolism takes flight,
Devi's abode, the feminine's embodiment of light.
Bhairagini Maas and Upasakas, guardians of the shrine,
Women tending to Devi, a tradition so divine.

Life energies transformed stone to deity's core,
Prana pratishtha's mystic lore.
Devi's energy structure, a rasa danda's chore,
Sadhguru's touch, the linga it bore.

In Yogic lore, Shiva in stillness lay,
Devi's touch, he awoke, a cosmic display.
Rudra's roar, creation's birth,
Devi's dance, the universe's mirth.

In emptiness, where darkness dwells,
Linga Bhairavi in silent spells.
From void to life, creation swells,
In her cosmic womb, the universe tells.

In the stillness and roar, in darkness she resides,
Linga Bhairavi, creation's silent guides.
From the sacred linga, cosmic energy flows,
In her embrace, devotion eternally glows.

Aadi

Shri Ayappa Swami of Sabarimala

In the hills of Sabarimala, where devotion ignites,
Ayyappa Swami, in spiritual heights.
Born of Shiva and Vishnu's cosmic blend,
In Ayyappa's grace, devotees find transcend.

A pilgrimage to Sabarimala's sacred peak,
Devotees in thousands, their vows they seek.
Mandala Kalam, a forty-one-day vow,
Austerities observed, devotion's sacred plough.

In the western ghats, where nature hums,
Ayyappa Swami, in devotion drums.
The unity of Shiva and Vishnu's lore,
Ayyappa's presence, in the pilgrim's core.

Scientifically, a convergence rare,
Shiva and Vishnu, a cosmic pair.
Ayyappa's essence, a unity profound,
In the cosmic dance, where mysteries abound.

Sabarimala, a tapestry divine,
Where Ayyappa's presence, in every shrine.
In the midst of nature's serene embrace,
Devotees find solace, in Ayyappa's grace.

Contributions to Hinduism, a pilgrimage grand,
Ayyappa's teachings, across the land.
Unity of faith, where hearts unite,
In Sabarimala's pilgrimage, devotion takes flight.

Through the hills and rivers, united masses tread,
A sacred journey to Sabarimala widespread.
In devotion's tapestry, threads interlace,
Connecting hearts, irrespective of caste and race.

Ayyappa's pilgrimage, a sacred bind,
In Sabarimala's journey, unity we find.
Indian masses, diverse yet one,
In the name of Ayyappa, under the sun.

Across the subcontinent, a sacred call,
Sabarimala's journey, breaking every wall.
In unity of devotion, where hearts converse,
Ayyappa's pilgrimage, a nation's diverse.

So in the hills of Sabarimala, devotion's fire,
Ayyappa Swami, the soul's desire.
Contributions vast, to the Hindu lore,
In Ayyappa's grace, devotion's galore.

In the sacred journey's unity, India's masses stand,
Connected by faith, in Ayyappa's land.

 Aadi

Mato Tipila – Kailash of Red Indians

In the land where the prairies whisper their tales,
Mato Tipila stands, where the spirit prevails.
A lonely mountain, in solitude sublime,
The Kailash of America, a beacon through time.

At the heart of the Red Indian lore,
Mato Tipila's energy, forevermore.
Vishuddhi chakra, the throat's pure flow,
A cascade of music, where stories grow.

On this sacred peak where echoes reside,
Red Indian songs find their rhythmic stride.
A cradle of civilization in the West,
Mato Tipila's spirit, eternally blessed.

In the Lakota's heart, a vision unfolds,
Mato Tipila, where history Molds.
A guardian of culture, a sentinel of the land,
On this sacred mountain, the Red Indians stand.

Through the ages, in the prairie's dance,
Mato Tipila's spirit, a sacred trance.
Songs rise like smoke, to the sky they soar,
From the throat chakra, a cultural core.

A melody of legends, a harmony grand,
Mato Tipila, where the Red Indians stand.
In the whispering winds and the rivers that flow,
Their stories on this mountain, in echoes bestow.

Kailash of America, Mato Tipila's name,
In the Red Indian heart, forever aflame.
A cradle of civilization, a sacred peak,
Where the throat chakra's music will forever speak.

 Aadi

BharatVarsh – Oldest Continuously Surviving Civilization

Maa Saraswati

Maa Saraswati, divine and fair,
In Vedic hymns, your presence is not rare.
Goddess of wisdom, knowledge's source,
In your grace, we find our course.

Vedas echo your sacred name,
Saraswati, eternal flame.
A river's flow, a cosmic stream,
In every scholar's cherished dream.

With veena's notes, your melody,
A symphony of harmony.
Your swan, a symbol, pure and white,
Guiding seekers toward the light.

In the realms of art, you dance,
Inspiring minds, a poetic trance.
Brush strokes on the canvas of creation,
A goddess of eloquence and oration.

Blessings upon the seeker's quest,
In your sanctuary, minds find rest.
Books and scrolls, your sacred shrine,
A reservoir of wisdom, truly divine.

Oh, Saraswati, in the scholar's nook,
In every verse, in every book.
Your grace flows in the poet's pen,
A river of words, again and again.

In classrooms and temples, your altars rise,
A beacon for the curious, the wise.
Maa Saraswati, in your embrace,
We find the truth, the boundless grace.

As the river of knowledge, you inspire,
In every student's heart, you light the fire.
Maa Saraswati, we sing your song,
In learning's embrace, we all belong.

 Aadi

Vedas

In realms of ancient whispers, mystic and profound,
The Vedas echo secrets, in cosmic cycles bound.
Sacred hymns, a celestial script unfurled,
Wisdom woven in verses, the essence of the world.

Rigveda, the hymn of hymns, chants the cosmic song,
Mantras dancing in the ether, where divinity belongs.
Sama-Veda, the melodic muse, a celestial symphony,
Chants of gods and cosmic forces, in celestial harmony.

Yajur-Veda, the sacred code, rituals inscribed,
A bridge 'twixt the finite and divine, where reverence is prescribed.
Atharva-Veda, the spellbinding lore, magic's ancient scroll,
Charms to mend, to heal, to seek, a mystic's sacred goal.

Brahman, the cosmic essence, in verses is enshrined,
From the cosmic dance of Shiva to Vishnu's form defined.
Upanishads, the mystic dialogues, in the heart of the Vedic sea,
Whispers of the infinite, in the seeker's soul, set free.

Vedic fire, Agni, in ritual flames ascends,
Agni, the messenger, between mortal and transcendent friends.
Soma, the sacred nectar, intoxicates the divine,
In Vedic hymns and rituals, a cosmic union to entwine.

From creation's cosmic breath to the cycle of rebirth,
Vedas unfold the mysteries, the profoundness of the earth.
Vedic seers, the Rishis, in meditation deep,
Unveiling cosmic secrets, in the silence, they keep.

Yugas, cycles, cosmic dance, the eternal cosmic rhyme,
Vedas weave the tapestry of space and fleeting time.
Rta, the cosmic order, in every hymn reverberates,
A sacred rhythm, in the heart of creation, resonates.

Vedas, the eternal whispers, from the dawn of time,
A hymn to the cosmic forces, in every soul they chime.
In the sacred verses, the cosmic truth unfurls,
Vedas, the mystical echoes, where the universe twirls.

 Aadi

Panchatantra: Wisdom's Timeless Tale

In the hush of ancient whispers, a sage did write,
Pandit Vishnu Sharma, in wisdom's twilight.
A tapestry of fables, Panchatantra's embrace,
A journey through morals, each tale a grace.

Panchatantra, the five-fold lore,
A treasure trove, wisdom to explore.
Mitralabha, the friends attained,
First discourse, where wisdom's gained.

Two crows, a tale of loss and gain,
In branches high, they played life's game.
Through laughter and strife, a moral true,
Panchatantra whispered lessons anew.

Panchatantra's echo, across the land,
A wisdom beacon, in storyteller's hand.
For generations, its tales unfurl,
A gem of wisdom for every boy and girl.

Mice and elephants, a kingdom grand,
In Panchatantra's tales, they stand.
From smallest to mightiest, lessons drawn,
In each tale, wisdom is dawned.

A weaver and a queen, a counsel spun,
Through Panchatantra, wisdom won.
The art of counsel, in tales arrayed,
In its verses, truths portrayed.

Across the subcontinent, its tales did roam,
From royal courts to humble home.
A guide for rulers, a teacher's delight,
Panchatantra's impact, a scholarly height.

Beyond the borders, it found its way,
Translated, cherished, in lands far away.
Panchatantra's morals, a universal art,
Sewn into the fabric of every heart.

In Panchatantra's verses, a legacy sealed,
A sage's wisdom, in stories revealed.
Pandit Vishnu Sharma, in tales so fine,
Left footprints in the sands of time.

 Aadi

Holi – Not Just a Festival of Colors

In the realm of colours, where joy takes flight,
Holi, the festival, brings hearts alight.
A celebration, vibrant and grand,
Uniting humanity, across the land.

As the sun sets on the last full moon,
Old woes in flames, a ritual boon.
A blaze of colours, a tapestry divine,
Holi heralds the arrival of springtime.

Red, the hue of fiery emotion's might,
Green whispers of envy, out of sight.
Yellow beams with joy, a radiant sun,
Pink blooms with love, when all is one.

Blue stretches wide, a vast, open sky,
White cradles peace as clouds drift by.
Saffron ignites sacrifice's flame,
Violet, the hue of wisdom's name.

Humanity, a canvas, colours array,
Each emotion, a distinct display.
Holi, the carnival of life's embrace,
Breaking barriers with vibrant grace.

In the playground of existence, diverse and free,
Children of Earth, a harmonious spree.
No distinctions in colours that sway,
Holi unifies in its colourful array.

Like emotions pure, a rainbow cascade,
Life's roles, in clarity, gracefully laid.
A father, a spouse, a citizen true,
In each role, colours bloom anew.

The bonfire of Holika, a tale unfolds,
Prahlada's devotion, a story that moulds.
Faith's power, a protective fire,
In every ember, a lesson to aspire.

Holi, a festival beyond mere cheer,
A reflection of life, crystal clear.
Harmony in diversity, a colourful decree,
In the tapestry of Holi, humanity is free.

 Aadi

Mewar

In the heart of Rajasthan's royal embrace,
Lies Mewar, a realm of timeless grace.
Where history whispers from every stone,
A tale of valor, a kingdom's throne.

Amidst the Aravallis, proud and grand,
Mewar's legacy, a storied land.
Udaipur, the city of lakes serene,
Where tales of chivalry are felt and seen.

Majestic palaces against the sky,
City Palace, where echoes fly.
Amar Vilas, the garden of delight,
Mewar's beauty bathed in soft moonlight.

Kumbhalgarh, a fortress bold,
Whose walls the tales of valor hold.
Mewar's pride, standing tall,
Guardian of history, amidst it all.

Chittorgarh, where legends reside,
The tales of Mewar, far and wide.
Vijay Stambh, reaching for the skies,
A symbol of courage that never dies.

Mewar's rulers, noble and wise,
In every stone, their spirit lies.
Maharanas, guardians true,
In Mewar's heart, they forever grew.

The lakes of Fateh Sagar, Pichola's expanse,
Reflecting Mewar's timeless dance.
Boat rides whisper tales untold,
In Udaipur's waters, history unfolds.

Mewar, where festivals blaze in hues,
Dressed in vibrant, joyful clues.
Gangaur, the women's festival bright,
Colors dance in Mewar's light.

A land where traditions warmly embrace,
Rich heritage, a timeless grace.
Mewar, where Rajput pride stands tall,
In every fort, in every wall.

The Mewar breeze, a melody,
Whispers of warriors strong and free.
In the heart of Rajasthan's regal art,
Mewar, a masterpiece, forever in the heart.

Aadi

Bundelkhand

In the heart of India, where legends intertwine,
Bundelkhand stands, a realm so divine.
A land of tales etched in history's sand,
A canvas of courage, it's Bundelkhand.

Amidst Vindhyachal's ancient embrace,
This realm holds stories, a cultural grace.
Where valour echoes through each rocky strand,
A saga unfolds in Bundelkhand.

Chandelas carved temples to the sky,
Khajuraho's beauty, where gods and mortals lie.
A testament to art, a legacy grand,
Whispers of aesthetics in Bundelkhand.

Jhansi, the fortress of the warrior queen,
Rani Lakshmibai, in history, is seen.
With a sword in hand, she took her stand,
A symbol of resilience in Bundelkhand.

Betwa's river, a companion true,
Reflects the tales of Bundel's valorous crew.
Chhatris and cenotaphs, a memorial band,
Guard the tales of heroes in Bundelkhand.

In the vast ravines, where secrets dwell,
Bundelkhand's spirit, no words can tell.
Nature and history, hand in hand,
Paint a vivid portrait of Bundelkhand.

Bundeli folk songs, a melodic delight,
Dance in the air on a starry night.
A symphony of culture, an ensemble unplanned,
Resonates through the soul of Bundelkhand.

Bundelkhand, where traditions sing,
A kaleidoscope of life, every offering.
Through folklore and fables, the past is fanned,
A treasure trove of stories in Bundelkhand.

So, let the verses echo, let the ballads ring,
In Bundelkhand's embrace, let stories spring.
A legacy of valour, a timeless brand,
Forever engraved in Bundelkhand.

 Aadi

A Proud Son of Bharat!

In the tapestry of time, where history unfolds, I stand,
a proud son of Bharat, where stories are told.
A land adorned with colours, a mosaic of diversity,
Blessed with the history of millenniums, a profound legacy.

From the sacred rivers that gracefully flow,
To the peaks that touch the heavens in a radiant glow.
In every grain of soil and whispering breeze,
I find the echoes of my roots, the ancient trees.

A kaleidoscope of cultures, languages, and art,
In the beating heart of Bharat, I play my part.
With valorous tales etched in every stone,
I am a testament to a heritage, proudly my own.

From the verses of Vedas to the hymns of unity,
I am the proud son of Bharat, in profound affinity.
Through struggles and triumphs, our spirit endures,
In the embrace of this soil, my identity assures.

The dance of traditions, the melody of unity,
I am a proud son of Bharat, bound by eternity.
In the land where every step echoes history,
I carry the flame of pride, a cherished legacy.

With gratitude for the sacrifices, for freedom earned,
In the lessons of resilience, my spirit is discerned.
I stand tall, shoulders broad, a reflection of my land,
For I am a proud son of Bharat, with a distinguished blend.

 Aadi

Great Indian Wrestling

Beneath the sun's fervent gaze, a sacred ring unfurls,
Indian wrestling, a dance of strength that swirls.
Bodies entwined, a testament to might,
In the soil's embrace, warriors unite.

Mud-clad echoes of tradition resound,
As pehalwans grapple, on hallowed ground.
A symphony of sweat, determination's call,
Indian wrestling, where spirits stand tall.

In the akhara's domain, a rhythmic chant,
Muscles weave tales, in each flex and pant.
Grit etched on faces, resilience in the air,
A canvas of struggle, where champions dare.

Guru's wisdom whispers through the dust,
The akhara, a temple where respect is a must.
In the clash of bodies, an ancient art unfolds,
Indian wrestling, where tales of valour are told.

From dawn's first light to the dusk's descent,
The wrestling pit bears witness, silent and intent.
A cultural embrace, a heritage so divine,
In the heart of battle, a spirit does shine.

Oh, Indian wrestling, in your spirited embrace,
Legends are sculpted, leaving an indelible trace.
A dance of strength, a warrior's sweet refrain,
In the arena of tradition, where honour shall remain.

 Aadi

Ruins of Kuldhara – A Saga of Sacrifices, Dignity and Honour!

In the winter of 2021, I had the privilege of exploring the enigmatic "Ghost village" known as Kuldhara, located near Jaisalmer in the state of Rajasthan, India. The atmosphere in the vicinity immediately struck me with a profound emotional resonance. The legend surrounding Kuldhara recounts a compelling tale.

It is said that Salim Singh, the prime minister of Jaisalmer state at that time, harboured a desire for the daughter of the village head. Undeterred by her lack of consent, he adamantly declared his intention to marry her. In response to this egregious violation of their autonomy, a consequential event unfolded on a fateful night in 1825. The residents of Kuldhara and the adjacent 83 villages clandestinely vanished into obscurity, leaving behind a ghostly emptiness.

The remnants of Kuldhara tell a poignant narrative of self-respect, honor, and the unyielding pride of its erstwhile inhabitants. The dilapidated structures in the village echo the profound loss and the enduring spirit of a community that chose to vanish rather than succumb to the dishonor imposed upon them. In essence, Kuldhara stands as a haunting testament to the resilience and dignity of a people unwilling to compromise their principles.

In the stillness of the night, a village packed its dreams,
For self-respect, they journeyed far, beneath the moon's soft beams.
They left behind their humble homes, their roots in sacred soil,
To seek a brighter future, amidst uncertainty and toil.

With courage in their weary hearts, they ventured on the road,
A caravan of hope and pride, their self-respect bestowed.
Each step they took, a testament, to honour and to pride,
In unity, they marched ahead, no hardships could divide.

Underneath the vast, starry dome,
They left their ancestral home.
For Salim Singh's unjust demand,
To safeguard honour, they took a stand.

In the moonlit hours, they chose to depart,
Leaving behind their homes and heart.
The sacred Shiva Linga cradled with care,
A village's dignity in the desert's lair.

Through the years, the ruins stand tall,
A testimony to a departure, a silent call.
The temple's silence, the wind's soft hymn,
In the village's absence, echoes swim.

Leaving trails of memories, in the land they called their own,
They carried stories, culture, and the seeds that would be sown.
A village that had immigrated, not in fear but with respect,
To build anew, to rise above, their self-worth to protect.

In distant lands, they would find a new community,
Preserving traditions, weaving dreams, with unwavering unity.
For self-respect, they took the step, in search of brighter days,
A village that migrated overnight, with hope and honour ablaze.

Aadi

Historical Legends of Bharat

Acharya Chanakya

In the tapestry of ancient lore, a sage of might,
A polymath's brilliance, in the scholar's light.
Chanakya, Kauṭilya, by many names known,
In the annals of wisdom, his seeds were sown.

Philosopher, strategist, economist, profound,
A royal advisor, in intellect renowned.
Arthashastra's architect, a treatise so divine,
Guiding realms with wisdom, through every line.

In the corridors of time, his legacy unfolds,
A precursor to economics, the story it holds.
Between the fourth and third century, they say,
Chanakya's brilliance lit wisdom's array.

Lost in Gupta's twilight, his works concealed,
Until the 20th century, when truth revealed.
A pioneer in politics, a mastermind's grace,
In India's history, a monumental embrace.

Around 321 BCE, a pivotal year,
Chandragupta's ascent, Chanakya held dear.
Mauryan Empire's foundation, his strategic play,
The chief advisor's wisdom, lighting the way.

To Bindusara, Chandragupta's wise son,
Chanakya's counsel, like a river, did run.
In the tapestry of empires, his influence carved,
A sage, a guide, in history's annals, preserved.

Chanakya's saga, a tale of intellect's might,
In the grand narrative, a luminary light.
Teacher, author, strategist, so versatile,
In India's wisdom, he rests, mile after mile.

 Aadi

Chandragupt Maurya

In the ancient annals of Magadha's might,
A tale unfolds, bathed in history's light.
Chandragupt Maurya, a sovereign's birth,
Founder of an empire, sweeping in girth.

Three fifty BCE marked his earthly debut,
A realm's architect, a vision so true.
From Pataliputra, the Nanda Empire's throne,
To Greek satraps, territories his own.

Against Alexander's ghost, he rose,
Defeating the Nanda, his triumph glows.
A victor over Greek dominion's reign,
Chandragupt, a monarch, breaking the chain.

Western borders secured, a frontier grand,
Seleucus, a rival, on the war-torn sand.
Two years of strife, the outcome foreseen,
A marriage pact, a truce serene.

From Bengal's embrace to Afghanistan's hold,
His empire's expanse, a saga retold.
North India's heart, Central's embrace,
Chandragupt's realm, a vast sovereign space.

Contrary to legends that time would unfold,
Brahminical rites in his reign still enrolled.
Hunting pursuits, far from Ahimsa's grace,
A warrior king, in life's vibrant race.

Economic boom, reforms profound,
Infrastructure's growth, the empire unbound.
Religious embrace, a tolerant hand,
Buddha's whispers, Brahman's command.

Zoroastrian echoes, Greek gods revered,
A tapestry woven, diverse and revered.
On Chandragiri's hill, a memorial stands,
A testament etched in the timeless sands.

Maurya's era, an age of might,
A beacon of progress, a cultural height.
Chandragupt Maurya, a visionary's dream,
In the vast canvas of history, a lasting gleam.

 Aadi

Baba Matsyendranath

In the ancient folds where mystic winds entwine,
A yogi emerged, Matsyendranath divine.
Bearing the wisdom of an age untold,
Shaping Bharat's spirit, a tale unfold.

Hatha yoga's guardian, a revival's spark,
In Matsyendra's gaze, a cosmic arc.
Traditions embraced him, both Buddhist and Hindu,
A saintly soul, with teachings anew.

Natha Sampradaya, he did ignite,
The flame of knowledge, pure and bright.
Guided by Shiva, in profound trance,
Matsyendranath, the yogic dance.

A Siddhar esteemed in Tamil Nadu's lore,
Machamuni, his presence evermore.
In the sanctum of Kasi Viswanathar's shrine,
His Jeeva Samadhi, an eternal sign.

Eighty-four mahasiddhas, in mystic embrace,
Avalokiteśvara, an embodiment of grace.
Guru of Gorakhnath, the yogic heir,
In Matsyendra's whispers, divinity's lair.

The political landscape, the spiritual thread,
Woven by Matsyendra, where realms are wed.
An incarnation revered, beyond earthly kin,
In Matsyendranath's essence, both worlds begin.

Through ages untold, his teachings unfold,
A yogi's journey, a tale retold.
Matsyendranath, in the cosmic stream,
A mystic poet, a yogic dream.

 Aadi

Adi Guru Shankara – Being who Shaped Bharat

In the realm where Vedas whisper and Upanishads sing,
A sage emerged, a harmonious hymn did he bring.
Adi Shankara, the luminary of ancient lore,
Shaping Bharat's soul, on wisdom's sacred shore.

Eighth-century echoes, in the tapestry of time,
A Vedic scholar and acharya, sublime.
Brahmasutrabhasya, his intellectual might,
Bhagavad Gita's essence, in his words took flight.

Over 300 texts, a legacy vast,
Yet attributions questioned, through scholarly contrast.
Commentaries and stotras, a fountainhead divine,
Adi Shankara's wisdom, an eternal shrine.

Advaita Vedanta, his guiding flame,
Jivatman's true identity, he aimed to proclaim.
Beyond rituals and rites, a liberating view,
Upanishads' essence, in his teachings grew.

An uncharted path, with Mahayana's trace,
Critiques and debates, in intellectual space.
Hindu, Buddhist, and Jain threads entwined,
A cosmic dance of Atman, Anatta, and Brahman aligned.

Shankara's influence, a disputed quest,
Until the 10th century, overshadowed, not addressed.
Maṇḍana Miśra's shadow cast,
Till the 11th century, when his brilliance bloomed at last.

Four mathas, monastic echoes resonate,
Dashanami order, by his vision consecrate.
A ruler-renunciate, on digvijaya's quest,
Across the subcontinent, wisdom he expressed.

Hagiographies paint a tale of divine,
Deifying Shankara in the 14th-century shrine.
Organizer of mathas, unifier of tradition,
Shankaracharya, a revered apparition.

In the corridors of time, Adi Shankara stands,
A sage who shaped Bharat with wisdom's hands.
Shankaracharya, a title embraced with grace,
In the eternal dance, his spirit finds a place.

 Aadi

Lalitaditya Muktapida

In the kingdom of Kashmir, where legends unfold,
Lalitaditya, a monarch, resplendent and bold.
Karkota's sovereign, in regal attire,
His tale, a saga, set the land on fire.

In Kalhana's verses, a "world conqueror" named,
Miraculous powers, conquests proclaimed.
Yashovarman defeated, central India at his feet,
To eastern and southern realms, his armies beat.

Through valleys and rivers, his banners unfurled,
A short-lived empire, across the world.
From Afghanistan's peaks to Central Asia's expanse,
Lalitaditya's rule, a cosmic dance.

In Parihasapura, a new capital did rise,
Amidst Srinagara's echoes, under azure skies.
Shrines commissioned, in devotion and might,
Martand's Sun Temple, a symphony of light.

A descendent claimed, of Nāga's royal line,
Karkotaka's blood, in Lalitaditya's spine.
Towns established, under his sovereign hand,
A king revered, in the timeless land.

Oh, Lalitaditya, in history enshrined,
Your tale echoes through time, in every kind.
A sovereign sage, a conqueror grand,
In Kashmir's embrace, your legacy stands.

 Aadi

Alha – Udal

In the heartlands of India, where legends take flight,
Echoes the saga of Alha and Udal, valiant and bright.
A tale woven in verses, of warriors so grand,
Alha-udal's story, across the land.

Born in the dust of a legendary soil, Alha,
with courage, began to embroil.
Udal, his brother, by loyalty entwined,
Together they stood, against fate's design.

Mahoba witnessed their valorous start,
An unyielding bond, a warrior's heart.
Chand Bardai, the poet, with quill and with ink,
Etched their epic, so the world could drink.

Rajput blood in their veins, the sword in their hand,
Alha-udal's courage, across the land.
Bundelkhand's pride, in tales they reside,
Against all odds, with a warrior's stride.

Bhaisasur's challenge, the mighty duel,
Alha-udal's valour, a saga to fuel.
Chittorgarh's siege, a battle so grand,
Alha-udal's strength, like shifting sand.

A tale of love, of loyalty and might,
In the moonlit fields, under the night.
Alha's devotion to Vimala so true,
Udal's love for Basmani, the skies knew.

Through battles and trials, they carved their fate,
A symphony of valour, woven innate.
Alha-udal's tale, a resounding song,
In the fabric of time, eternally strong.

In Bundelkhand's echoes, their names endure,
Alha-udal's legacy, forever pure.
A saga of courage, in history's braid,
Alha-udal's story, never to fade.

 Aadi

Maharana Pratap

Beneath the Rajputana sun, where legends breathe,
Maharana Pratap, a lion unsheathed.
On Mewar's throne, a sovereign's might,
Valiant heart, a beacon in the fight.

In the annals of valour, his tale is inscribed,
A warrior's spirit, in battles described.
Against the Mughals, a steadfast stand,
Maharana Pratap, guardian of his land.

At Haldighati's pass, a battlefield's stage,
Rajput valour etched on history's page.
Mounted on Chetak, his loyal steed,
A saga of courage, a knightly creed.

In the face of adversity, a lion's roar,
Mewar's resolute defender, forevermore.
Through rugged terrains and trials untold,
Maharana Pratap's story unfolds.

A symbol of honour, in each sword's gleam,
Maharana's valour, a timeless stream.
Against the tides of time, a hero stands,
Maharana Pratap, pride of Rajput lands.

 Aadi

Goswami Tulsidas

In the realm of devotion, where verses unfold,
Goswami Tulsidas, a poet of gold.
Born in the 16th century's embrace,
His words resonate, a spiritual grace.

Ramcharitmanas, his magnum opus divine,
A poetic narrative, where virtues entwine.
In the heart of Ayodhya, the tale unfurls,
Tulsidas' devotion, in poetic pearls.

A devotee of Lord Rama, with love so deep,
His words in devotion, a vow to keep.
Ram Bhakti, the essence of his lore,
In verses profound, a spiritual core.

Hanuman Chalisa, a hymn of might,
In forty verses, devotion takes flight.
Lord Hanuman's glory, in rhythmic song,
Tulsidas' devotion, strong and strong.

Contributions to the Bhakti wave,
In devotion's ocean, his verses pave.
Bridge to the divine, in poetic art,
Tulsidas' words, a spiritual heart.

For the Indian subcontinent, a guiding light,
In Tulsidas' verses, truth takes flight.
Hinduism's tapestry, he intricately wove,
A beacon of love, in devotion's trove.

In Ayodhya's soil, his devotion sown,
Tulsidas' legacy, forever known.
A poet, philosopher, wrestler, a sage so grand,
For the soul of India, a guiding hand.

In devotion's garden, his verses bloom,
Tulsidas' wisdom, dispelling gloom.
For Hinduism, a luminous gem,
In his poetic hymns, we find the realm.

So in the pages of history, his ink inscribed,
Goswami Tulsidas, devotion prescribed.
A sage, a poet, his contributions vast,
In the spiritual journey, a guide steadfast.

 Aadi

Chhatrapati Shivaji Maharaj

In the heart of the Deccan, a lion roared,
Chhatrapati Shivaji, a name adored.
With valour ablaze, a lion's might,
He carved a kingdom, a beacon of light.

Born of the soil, a son of the land,
In the Maratha veins, courage grand.
Against oppression, a steadfast stand,
Shivaji rose, a hero so grand.

A strategist keen, in warfare wise,
On the battlefield, his spirit flies.
Mountain forts, like sentinels high,
Guardians of freedom 'neath the sky.

Fearless heart, a warrior's grace,
In the tumult of battle, a lion's embrace.
Sworn to protect, with a sovereign gaze,
Shivaji's realm, where dharma stays.

Hindavi Swaraj, his noble quest,
To uphold justice, he gave his best.
A realm of justice, where all find rest,
In Shivaji's kingdom, they were blessed.

Against the tide of tyrants bold,
Shivaji stood, his spirit untold.
From Bijapur's might, to Mughal's decree,
He defied them all, for his people's glee.

Raigad's throne, a symbol high,
Where the lion roared beneath the sky.
A leader true, for whom people sigh,
Chhatrapati Shivaji, never say die.

Maratha Empire, a legacy vast,
Shivaji's vision, forever cast.
In every fort and stone steadfast,
The lion's echoes, in history, last.

With justice as armour and courage as sword,
Chhatrapati Shivaji, a name adored.
In the heart of Bharat, his spirit soared,
A lion-king, by history, crowned and stored.

Amidst the rugged terrains and battles untold,
Shivaji, the lion, a saga unfolds.
Through the Deccan's embrace, a warrior's quest,
Fighting battles, putting valour to the test.

Pratapgad's roar echoed in the hills,
Where Afzal Khan's might met Shivaji's skills.
A single stroke, a daring feat,
The lion prevailed, in victory sweet.

Panhala's fortress, a bastion tall,
Against Siddi Johar, who sought its fall.
With strategic brilliance, Shivaji stood,
Defending his land, the lionhood.

In the heart of Raigad, the coronation's call,
Challenging Bijapur, he stood tall.
Under the crescent moon, an empire's birth,
Shivaji's valour echoed in every hearth.

The siege of Purandar, a tale profound,
A test of resilience, the Maratha crown.
Shivaji, undeterred, faced each blow,
His spirit unbroken, a warrior's glow.

Rairi's conquest, a strategic gain,
Against the Adilshahi, he would not feign.
Through battles fierce, in the Maratha name,
Shivaji's lionheart burned with flame.

Kondana's fort, now known as Sinhagad,
Witnessed valor, where Shivaji led.
Against the Mughals, a lion's stand,
Defending the soil, the Maratha land.

Through the tapestry of battles bold,
Shivaji's saga, a legend told.
Against tyrants, with courage untold,
The lion-king, his people consoled

 Aadi

Comprehending Comprehensions

A Painting

Upon a canvas, colours come alive,
In strokes and hues, emotions do thrive.
A painter's soul, with every stroke they dive,
Creating worlds where dreams and realities collide.

With each brush dipped in a sea of thought,
The artist's vision, a masterpiece is sought.
From darkest shadows to the light they've brought,
In the heart of a painting, a story is caught.

A silent dialogue in pigments and shade,
A story untold, in the colours displayed.
In the canvas, secrets are laid,
In the depths of a painting, emotions cascade.

Each stroke reveals a piece of the heart,
A glimpse of the artist's life, a unique art.
In the tapestry of colours, where worlds depart,
A painting speaks, a silent work of heart.

So, let us wander through this painted land,
Where feelings and thoughts are brushed by hand.
In the realm of a painting, we understand,
The language of the soul, where emotions expand.

Aadi

A Failed Attempt

In the quiet echoes of a failed endeavour's hush,
Dreams crumble like autumn leaves in a gentle crush.
Bold ambitions, a fragile castle in the sand,
Yet destiny had different cards in its guiding hand.

A dance with hope, a waltz with aspirations high,
Yet reality's dissonance sings a sombre lullaby.
Striving for the summit, but stumbling on the slope,
A canvas of efforts, brushed with dreams, elopes.

In the wreckage of attempts, resilience finds its voice,
Lessons etched in scars, a narrative of choice.
A symphony of setbacks, a chorus of defeat,
Yet within each falter, seeds of strength discreet.

Oh, the echoes of failure, a bitter, poignant song,
Yet within its verses, the resilient heart grows strong.
For in the tapestry of setbacks, woven with threads of grace,
A phoenix rises from the ashes, embracing a new embrace.

Aadi

Israel – Abode of Jews

In a land where history's tales reside,
Israel's beauty, its people's pride.
A nation with stories, ancient and wide,
In its landscapes and cities, cultures coincide.

From the desert's edge to the Mediterranean shore,
Israel's wonders, you can't ignore.
Mountains that rise, history galore,
In every step, its essence we explore.

Jerusalem's streets, where traditions blend,
A city with stories that never end.
In the Old City, prayers ascend,
Israel's spirit, a message to send.

From Tel Aviv's beaches to Galilee's calm,
Israel's diversity, a soothing balm.
In the fields where kibbutzim farm,
The heart of Israel, a peaceful psalm.

Innovation's cradle, where dreams take flight,
A startup nation, reaching new height.
Israel's future, so brilliantly bright,
In its accomplishments, a guiding light.

A nation of hope, resilience, and grace,
In this sacred land, many find their place.
Israel's spirit, an enduring embrace,
A tapestry of cultures, a harmonious space.

Aadi

Indori Poha

In the heart of India, where flavours entwine,
A cultural symphony, a breakfast divine.
Upon the streets of Indore, in the morning's light,
Awakens the aroma of Indori Poha, a culinary delight.

In the bustling bazaars, where vendors call,
The magic of spices, a taste for all.
Puffed rice adorned with savoury glee,
A heritage dish, a cultural decree.

Turmeric's warmth, a golden hue,
Mirch's spice, a flavour that's true.
Mustard seeds pop, a tiny percussion,
In the cauldron of culture, a breakfast fusion.

Curry leaves dance, a fragrant ballet,
Mixed with onions, at the break of day.
Tantalizing aromas, a sensory spree,
Indori Poha, a cultural legacy.

Sprinkled with sev, a crunchy grace,
A garnish that crowns, a flavourful embrace.
Accompanied by jalebi's sweet affair,
A symphony on the palate, beyond compare.

In every grain, a tale is spun,
Of Indore's streets, kissed by the sun.
A cultural journey on a breakfast plate,
Indori Poha, where flavours congregate.

 Aadi

Plight of Red Indians

Beneath the vast expanse of prairies so wide,
A tale unfolds, of a people's silent stride.
Red Indians, with spirits strong and free,
Their history etched in pain and tragedy.

Once, a harmonious dance with nature's song,
They lived where ancient spirits belong.
A vibrant tapestry of tribes so grand,
A culture rooted in this sacred land.

Then came the ships with sails unfurled,
An intrusion into their tranquil world.
The Europeans, seeking wealth and power,
Brought forth a storm, a fatal hour.

Through the whispers of the winds, they came,
A force that would never be the same.
The Red Indians, guardians of the earth,
Faced a foe with hunger for gold and hearth.

Lands usurped, like a thief in the night,
Promises broken, hopes taking flight.
Trail of Tears, a mournful track,
A forced march, with hearts so black.

Brutality stained the sacred ground,
As European greed knew no bound.
Blood-soaked chapters of history unfold,
A tragedy untold, a story of old.

Their spirits soared, but the price was high,
As ancestral echoes echoed a mournful cry.
The Red Indians, a people so wise,
Faced a fate where dignity dies.

Yet, in the embers of their struggle and strife,
A resilient flame, a flicker of life.
The spirit endures, though history weeps,
For the Red Indians, in memory, sleeps.

In the shadows of the sunset's glow,
Whispers linger, of a people who know.
Their history erased, yet spirits remain,
In the echoes of sorrow, in the winds' refrain.

Aadi

Deed of Most Intelligent – Weapons of Mass Destruction

In the shadows of progress, a sinister tale,
Of weapons of mass destruction, a dark travail.
Nuclear bombs, born of human creation,
A haunting legacy, a brutal manifestation.

In the annals of history, Hiroshima's lament,
A city obliterated, in a moment's descent.
The mushroom cloud, a harbinger of doom,
A spectre of destruction, an impending gloom.

Radiation whispers, a silent killer's song,
Lingering for generations, an insidious wrong.
Cancerous echoes, diseases untold,
A legacy of destruction, in history's fold.

Nagasaki's sorrow, etched in the ash,
A symphony of horror, a desolate clash.
In the aftermath, where shadows loom,
Generations scarred, in the nuclear tomb.

Chernobyl's tragedy, a nuclear dance,
A catastrophic echo, a deadly trance.
Radiation seeping through the soil and air,
A poisoned legacy, beyond repair.

Environmental hazards, a planet in despair,
Ecosystems shattered, a world laid bare.
The ozone weeps, as forests decline,
In the aftermath of mankind's design.

Yet, why, oh why, would humans create,
Such destructive forces, sealing their fate?
A dance with shadows, a deadly embrace,
In the pursuit of power, a moral disgrace.

In the halls of science, where knowledge resides,
A choice to wield destruction or to cast it aside.
The question lingers, a haunting reflection,
Why unleash weapons of mass destruction?

For in the dreadful aftermath, we find,
A plea for peace, a collective mind.
To protect our world, and its fragile connection,
Against the horrors of mass destruction.

 Aadi

Royal Enfield – Queen of Roads

In the kingdom of thunderous echoes, a steel steed,
Royal Enfield rides with a regal stampede.
Chrome gleams like armour in the morning light,
A symphony of pistons, a majestic flight.

Through winding roads and tales untold,
The Royal Enfield, a legacy to unfold.
Thumping heartbeat on asphalt trails,
A saga of freedom, where the wind prevails.

In the saddle, a rider dons a crown of leather,
A journey scripted in every rev, an adventure tethered.
Handlebars, like sceptres, guiding the way,
Royal Enfield, a monarch of the highway.

Beneath the sun's embrace, a metallic gleam,
Unveiling stories, like pages in a dream.
A mechanical soul with a nostalgic feel,
Royal Enfield, a ride that time can't steal.

Oh, the thunderous roar, a royal decree,
As the open road cradles both rider and destiny.
In the symphony of gears, a timeless appeal,
Royal Enfield, a monarch on two wheels.

 Aadi

Police Inspector

In the shadows of the city's heartbeat, where sirens wail,
A police inspector stands, clad in justice's mail.
Eyes that carry the weight of countless nights,
A sentinel of order, in city lights.

In the echoes of footsteps on a midnight street,
A police inspector walks, a guardian discreet.
Badge gleaming, a symbol of authority,
In the labyrinth of crime, a beacon of clarity.

Through the alleys of danger, where shadows creep,
A sworn protector, in the city's sleep.
A coat of valour, with sleeves rolled tight,
A police inspector marches through the night.

With each case, a piece of their soul they lend,
In the pursuit of truth, they never bend.
A symphony of sirens, a pulse of law,
In the inspector's gaze, justice raw.

Yet, behind the stoic facade they wear,
A heart that feels, burdened by care.
For in the quest for order, emotions blend,
A police inspector, a guardian and friend.

Oh, the police inspector, with a heart of steel,
In the tapestry of justice, they eternally kneel.
In the city's heartbeat, their duty calls,
A protector of peace, as the darkness falls

 Aadi

Samyama

In the heart of stillness, where silence reigns,
Samyama with Sadhguru, where the soul gains.
Ten days unfold, a sacred dance,
In the embrace of grace, a mystical trance.

Three days of Aum, Namah Shivaaya's call,
Echoing through the ashram walls.
Vibrations entwined, in cosmic rhyme,
A dance with divinity, transcending time.

Six months in preparation, ashram's hold,
A seeker's journey, a story untold.
Eligible to enter the sacred space,
Samyama beckons, a divine embrace.

Ten days of silence, a profound retreat,
Where the heart and breath in unity meet.
In the cocoon of stillness, shadows unfold,
Breath consciousness, a tale to be told.

A dance with the breath, a cosmic flow,
In the silence, the secrets of existence glow.
Sadhguru's guidance, a beacon bright,
Illuminating the path in the silent night.

Amidst this journey, a bond grows strong,
With Dhyanalinga, where hearts belong.
A silent communion, in the linga's embrace,
A sacred connection, a timeless space.

Breath-conscious, the spirit takes flight,
In the presence of the Guru, a sacred light.
Ten days, unexplainable, a timeless trance,
Samyama with Sadhguru, a mystical dance.

In the quietude, where words dissolve,
A bonding with Dhyanalinga, problems resolve.
A journey within, where the self unwinds,
Samyama's magic in the seeker's minds.

Ten days unfold, a sacred space,
In Samyama's grace, a divine embrace.
Breath-conscious, in the cosmic stream,
A seeker's journey, a mystical dream.

Aadi

Acknowledgements

In the symphony of life, where eternal reverberations find their tune, my heart overflows with thanks to those who have been the notes and melodies in my journey.

To Isha Foundation and Sadhguru Shri Jaggi Vasudev, whose profound teachings and transformative practices have illuminated my path, guiding me towards self-discovery and inner well-being. Your wisdom has been the North Star in the tapestry of my existence.

To the Hyderabad Runners Society, where the rhythm of my footsteps merged with the collective heartbeat of a running community. The miles we traversed together, the shared victories, and the unspoken camaraderie shaped not just my fitness but my spirit.

To all the individuals, experiences, and moments that I encountered in this beautiful journey—each a brushstroke in the painting of my life. To the ones who challenged me, the ones who supported me, and the ones who simply passed through, leaving an indelible mark.

To my family—the pillars of my strength and the keepers of my roots. To my father, whose love and teachings continue to guide me, even in his physical absence. To my mother, whose nurturing embrace is my sanctuary. To my younger brother, Avani, a beacon of innocence and purity. To my sisters, Moksha and Kshama, who truly embody the essence of liberation and forgiveness.

A special acknowledgment to the blessings of my ancestors and forefathers, whose unseen hands have shaped the trajectory of my life. Though not present in the physical realm, their influence and guidance are palpable in every step I take.

This book, 'Eternal Reverberations,' is not just mine; it belongs to the intricate dance of connections and influences that have coloured my world. Thank you all for being a part of this symphony.

About the Author

Aditya is A Fusion of Tech Mastery, Fitness Passion, Yogic energy, Mythological Insight, Love for History, and Artistic Talent. A seasoned tech product enthusiast, tech influencer, ultra marathoner, yoga practitioner, mythologist, author, an ardent traveller and a history buff with over a decade in software product management. A versatile leader, Aditya has crafted and scaled innovative B2B products, showcasing a unique blend of tech prowess, leadership, and a rich tapestry of interests.

Meet Aditya:

Holistic Lifestyle: An avid ultra marathon runner, yoga practitioner, and fitness influencer, Aditya is committed to physical, mental and spiritual well-being for the greater good.

Mythological Lens: Aditya intertwines mythologies with modern tech and sciences, offering a unique perspective on the ancient and contemporary.

History Enthusiast: With a love for history, Aditya explores culturally rich sites globally, connecting the dots between mythology, history, science and technology deriving a distinguished perspective on WHY, HOW and What part of the equation for human civilization.

Artistic Flair: Aditya showcases his artistic talent through captivating landscapes and performing vocals of Sanskrit chants, adding a creative touch to his diverse skill set.

Sportsman: Proficient in lawn tennis, chess, and cricket, Aditya's love for sports mirrors his strategic thinking and competitive spirit.

Product Maestro: Aditya navigates the entire product lifecycle, launching high-ROI products and leading top-performing teams.

Community Contributor: Beyond the corporate realm, Aditya is an active contributor to society. His involvement with the Isha Foundation of Sadhguru Jaggi Vasudeva and the Hyderabad Runners Society reflects his commitment to giving back. Aditya also shares his wealth of knowledge by occasionally writing and speaking on various topics related to product management & technical innovations, Ancient Indian history and wisdom, running and holistic wellbeing at various industry-recognized platforms.

Leadership Excellence: A natural collaborator, Aditya builds and mentors top-tier engineering teams, showcasing organizational and management finesse.

Authorship Journey: As Aditya delves into authorship, his book promises a rich tapestry of science, fitness, mythology, history, patriotism and artistic expression, offering readers a holistic experience.

Linkedin.com/in/adityapandeyadi

Facebook.com/Aditya.pandey.31105

x.com/Pandey_Aadityaa

Instagram.com/adityaveshpandey

www.ingramcontent.com/pod-product-compliance
Lightning Source LLC
LaVergne TN
LVHW041108150826
845673LV00007B/1965

9798892776684